Saxophones

Music Makers

THE CHILD'S WORLD®, INC.

Saxophones

Sharon Sharth

THE CHILD'S WORLD®, INC.

On the cover: This saxophone ends with a shiny metal bell.

The Child's World

Published in the United States of America by The Child's World®, Inc.
PO Box 326
Chanhassen, MN 55317-0326
800-599-READ
www.childsworld.com

Product Manager Mary Berendes
Editor Katherine Stevenson, Ph.D.

Library of Congress Cataloging-in-Publication Data
Sharth, Sharon.
Saxophones / by Sharon Sharth.
        p. cm.
Includes index.
ISBN 1-56766-044-4 (lib. bdg. : alk. paper)
1. Saxophone—Juvenile literature. [1. Saxophone.]   I. Title.
ML975 .S53 2002
788.7'19—dc21
                                    2001005997

Photo Credits
© CORBIS: 23 (base flute, bassoon, clarinet, flute, oboe, recorder)
© Gary Conner/IndexStock: 10
© Henry Diltz/CORBIS: 13
© Kelly-Mooney Photography/CORBIS: 15
© Kurt Stier/CORBIS: cover, 2
© Mitchell Gerber/CORBIS: 9
© PhotoDisc: 23 (pan flute, piccolo, slide whistle)
© Richard Cummins/CORBIS: 16, 19
© Stuart Westmorland/CORBIS: 6
© Underwood & Underwood/CORBIS: 20

Table of Contents

Chapter	Page
The Saxophone	7
What Is a Saxophone?	8
Different Kinds of Saxophones	11
What Shape Are Saxophones?	12
The Mouthpiece	14
The Keys	17
Playing the Saxophone	18
Jazz Saxophone	21
Sounds of the Saxophone	22
Other Woodwind Instruments	23
Glossary and Index	24

You hear its joyful cry at football games when the marching band strolls by. You hear it wail in jazz bands and growl on television and in films. What instrument is almost as expressive as the human voice? It's the saxophone!

What Is a Saxophone?

A saxophone is a musical instrument made of metal, usually brass. It is part of a group of instruments called **woodwinds**. Woodwind instruments make sound when you blow air through them. You can make different sounds by covering or opening the holes on the tube, or body, of the instrument. Oboes and flutes are woodwinds, too.

Here performer Kenny G sets the world record ➡ for playing the longest saxophone note.

9

soprano saxophones

alto saxophone

baritone saxophone

tenor saxophone

10

Different Kinds of Saxophones

The saxophone, or "sax," was invented over 160 years ago by Adolphe Sax, a Belgian instrument maker. Saxophones come in five different sizes. The bass saxophone is the largest and plays the lowest sounds, or **notes**. The highest notes come from the smallest sax, the soprano saxophone. Between these two are the alto, tenor, and baritone saxophones. The alto and tenor are the most popular saxophones to play.

← Here you can see some of the different kinds of saxophones.

What Shape Are Saxophones?

A saxophone is shaped a little like a letter S. Besides a saxophone's tubelike body, it has a **mouthpiece** at one end. The other end curves upward and is shaped like a bell. Saxophones with a longer body can play lower notes. Saxophones with a shorter body can play higher notes. That is why baritone and soprano saxophones sound so different!

Soprano saxophones also have a different shape. Their straight body makes them look something like a clarinet.

You can see the curved body of this tenor saxophone. ➔

The Mouthpiece

To play a saxophone, you blow air through the metal mouthpiece. A single, flat **reed** is attached to the mouthpiece. The reed makes a sound as it **vibrates**, or moves back and forth, against the mouthpiece.

To make the right kind of sounds, you must blow directly into the mouthpiece. Don't let the air escape! You must also make sure the reed is moist. If it is dry, it can't vibrate, and the sax will squeak.

You can see how this sax player is blowing air into the mouthpiece. He is playing at the Chicago Blues Festival. →

The saxophone's tubelike body has 20 holes. A small, padded flap covers each hole when you press a button, or **key**. When most of the holes are open, the saxophone can play higher notes. Closing more holes produces lower notes.

← You can see the keys on this saxophone.

Playing the Saxophone

To play a saxophone, you hold it in front of you with your fingers resting lightly on the keys. Then you blow air into the mouthpiece to make the reed vibrate. The air moves through the body of the sax. You push the keys to open and close the holes. Opening and closing the holes changes where the air can come out. That determines how high or low the notes will be.

This woman is playing a saxophone in a street band. ➡

19

Jazz Saxophone

The saxophone is popular in jazz music. One of the most famous American jazz saxophone players was Charlie Parker. His nickname was "Bird," and he could make his saxophone sing like one. He played the alto sax and helped create a new style of music called bebop. Bebop music is based on making up sounds, or **improvising**, in front of the audience.

Sounds of the Saxophone

A saxophone can make many of the same sounds you can make with your voice. It can sing, laugh, and even scream! A saxophone can sound brassy and loud. It can sound soothing and gentle. You can play pop, jazz, and classical music on a sax. Would you like to play the saxophone?

Other Woodwind Instruments

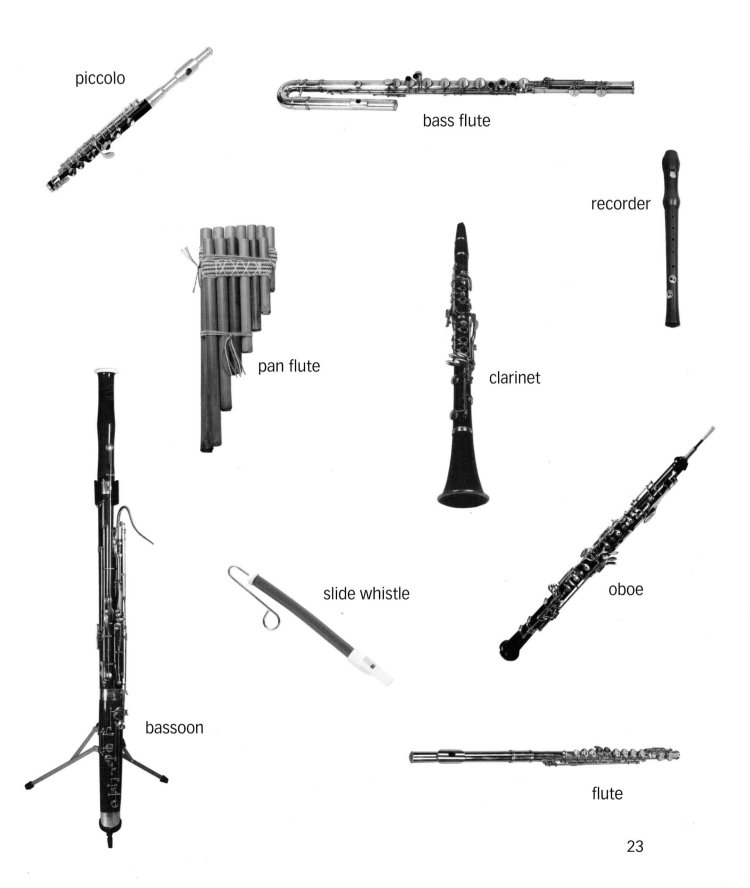

piccolo

bass flute

recorder

pan flute

clarinet

bassoon

slide whistle

oboe

flute

Glossary

improvising (IM-pruh-vy-zing)
Improvising is making something up as you go along. Improvising is a big part of some kinds of jazz music, such as bebop.

key (KEEZ)
On a saxophone, keys are small buttons you press to cover holes along the saxophone's body. Saxes have keys.

mouthpiece (MOWTH-peece)
The mouthpiece is the part of an instrument where you hold your mouth to play. Blowing air through the mouthpiece produces sound.

notes (NOHTS)
A note is a musical sound. Pressing the keys on a saxophone produces different notes.

reed (REED)
On some instruments, including saxophones, a reed is a thin piece of wood, metal, or plastic fastened to the mouthpiece. Blowing air into the mouthpiece moves the reed and makes a sound.

vibrates (VY-brates)
When something vibrates, it moves back and forth very quickly. Blowing into a saxophone mouthpiece makes the reed vibrate against the mouthpiece.

woodwinds (WOOD-windz)
Woodwinds are tube-shaped musical instruments that you play by blowing air through them. Saxophones are woodwinds.

Index

alto saxophone, 11, 21

appearance, 8, 12

baritone saxophone, 11

bass saxophone, 11, 12

bebop, 21

body, 8, 12, 17, 18

clarinet, 12

flute, 8

history, 11

holding, 18

holes, 8, 17, 18

improvising, 21

jazz, 7, 21, 22

keys, 17, 18

mouthpiece, 12, 14, 18

notes, 11, 17, 18

oboe, 8

Parker, Charlie, 21

parts, 8

playing, 8, 14, 18

reed, 14, 18

Sax, Adolphe, 11

sizes, 11

soprano saxophone, 11, 12

sounds, 7, 11, 12, 14, 17, 18, 21, 22

tenor saxophone, 11

vibrates, 14, 18

woodwinds, 8